NICENE CANONS IN THE OLD NUBIAN LANGUAGE

Francis Llewellyn Griffith

Introduction by: D.P. Curtin

Dalcassian
Publishing
Company

PHILADELPHIA, PA

ISBN: 978-1-960069-86-3 (Paperback)

Library of Congress Control Number:
Author: Curtin, D.P. (1985-)

Printed by Ingram Content Group, 1 Ingram Blvd, La Vergne, Tennessee

First printing edition 2018.

Introduction

The Canons of the Council of Nicaea are by no means obscure. Any major branch of Catholicism or Orthodoxy, as well as some episopal branches of Protestantism, recite a variant of the creed each Sunday. Moreover, with the success of Dan Brown's best-known novel, there are now scores of pseudo-histories and conspiracy theories relating to the First Council of Nicaea. Its fame was perhaps even more pronounced in the late Classical world, where an ecumenical council of the church was something unparalleled in human history. Nation-states of the time did not hold large representative legislatures wherein members from an extended territory would meet to discuss matters of polity and philosophy. Institutions like the Roman Senate were political bodies, but they never functioned in this manner, despite the highest of republican hopes in the early Roman state. Constantine's assembly at Nicaea was therefore a novelty, something that was on the minds and lips of every Roman citizen, christian or pagan.

That said, the council presented a glaring issue within the Roman state: What happened to Christians outside of the jurisdiction of Rome? This issue would be dealt with more acutely in the West in the coming century as the edifice of Roman power crumbled, but the east was already struggling with this question. The kingdom of Armenia had recently converted to Christianity under St. Gregory the Illuminator in 301 AD, and the Kingdom of Axum had done likewise under St. Frumentius. Both states were independent of Roman suzerainty and had their own source of ecclesiastical authority: Were they then subject to the canons of Nicaea? Even some seventeen centuries later, that answer is mixed, as the Armenian Apostalic Church and the Ethiopian Orthodox Church do accept First Nicaea as authoritative, but the Assyrian Church of the East does not.

It might be worth giving some additional context, as the Christians within the Persian Empire, Rome's single largest rival, were directly impacted by this question of jurisdiction. What is more, the great persecution under Shapur II exacerbated the issue, as Christians were perceived as having potential loyalty to a council conveyed by a Roman emperor. Christians in Persia were therefore subjected to suspicion for the remainder of the 4th century. The Persian Emperor Yazdegerd (d. 421) sought to reverse this national policy by pursuing a middle course. Zoroastrianism would remain the state religion of the Persian state, and Christian would be allowed to practice unhindered, but they must do so under the auspices of a Persian church, the organization of which remained under the Persian crown. In 410 AD, the Persian bishops were allowed to meet at the Council of Seleucia-Ctesiphon, which was then the capital of the Sassanid Persian Empire. Among the various points it discussed were: the establishment of the Persian Church (Assyrian Church of the East); the definition of ecclesiastical provinces within the empire; the appointment of a 'Catholicos' or head of the church; and the approval of the canons rendered in Nicaea.

The fragments of the canons which survive in this document appear to be sourced originally in the Persian church, although the exact means of transmission is not clear. Based on the transliteration of certain names, there is a heavy Arabic influence present in the text. Moreover, the few elements that survive appear to address a dispute between the Nubian/Ethiopian bishops and their Persian counterparts. Attempting to grant a specific date for the composition of these texts is therefore a challenge, perhaps ranging from the 7th to 9th centuries. As they include various apocryphal canons from the original edicts at Nicaea, they are often referred to as the Pseudo-Nicene canons, or Arabic Nicene canons. On either account they are generally considered to be spurious, and the work of a later writer. However, they are not extant in any form.

This small book contains two large fragments which were translated by Francis Griffith over a century ago. The latter was found in a codex with the text of the Miracle of St. Mena, an older Coptic work. It has been speculated that these two texts shared some common relationship, but there appears to be little evidence to support this, as only the fragments of a dozen Nubian church texts survive. Speculating on relationships between texts is therefore subject to significant interpolation. What this text does give insight into is the relationship between apostolic churches outside of the Roman Empire, something that is rarely discussed by the church fathers, and which is rarely found except in fragmentary form.

D.P. Curtin
Dec. 26, 2017
Wexford, PA

FRAGMENT I

Canon 36. That the Ethiopians ought neither to create nor to elect a patriarch, because, on the contrary, their prelate should be under the authority of him who holds the see of Alexandria[1]. There may be among them one in place of the patriarch and should be called '*catholicos*'[2], because he has neither the honor nor the authority of the patriarch[3].

If it happens that a council be convened and that the prelate of the Ethiopians be present, let him take the seventh place, after the prelate of Seleucia[4].

---

[1] The Ethiopian church holds a tradition that their Abuna, or Archbishop, goes back to St. Frumentius in the 4th century. However, historically, their church authorities stem from the early 7th century with the expulsion of the so-called Nine Saints.

[2] This is a title not uncommonly used in the Eastern Syriac rite and the Armenian church. Its utilization here is confusing, as a Catholicos is usually the head of the nation's orthodox church.

[3] It is possible that the Ethiopians that the alleged council is concerned with are in fact Nubians, as the Axumite bishops have their authority at least partially defined by the 8th century.

[4] It is unclear what Ecumenical Council this would be, unless there were African delegates at the Council of Seleucia-Ctesiphon in 410 AD. The jurisdiction claimed by the Church of the East at the time was any Christian outside of the boundaries of the Roman Empire.

If the authority is given to him to create archbishops in his province, he will not, however, be permitted to appoint any of them [Ethiopians]. If anyone does not obey, the Synod will excommunicate him.

Canon 42. That the Ethiopians should not appoint a patriarch from among their learned men, because he is to be appointed under the authority of the Alexandrian patriarch, to whom it pertains to ordain and appoint for them a "catholicos", who is inferior to the patriarch. The aforesaid, established with the name of "*catholicos*", will not be permitted to appoint archbishops as the patriarch does, because he is given only the name and honor of the patriarch, but not the true authority[5].

If it happens that a Synod be called in the land of the Rūm[6], and that this prelate be present, he should take his seat in the eighth place[7], after the lord of Seleucia, which is Almodayen[8], for this prelate has the authority of creating bishops for his province, while it has been forbidden [to the Ethiopian] to appoint anyone of them [Ethiopians].

Whosoever transgresses this order, the Fathers of the Synod will excommunicate him.

---

[5] Given the frequency and repetition of this canon it must be assumed that there was a controversy relating to the election and establishment of bishops. It is possible that this was a reaction to the growing autonomy of the Ethiopian church under Minas of Axum.

[6] The arabic transliteration of Rome, that is 'the Roman Empire'.

[7] This appears to be built on the ecclesiastical theory of the Pentarchy, with additional eastern sympathies. The rank of bishops according to this tract would be: 1) Rome, 2) Constantinople, 3) Alexandria, 4) Antioch, 5) Jerusalem, 6) Etchmiadzin, 7) Seleucia-Ctesiphon, 8) Axum

[8] This grants us a terminus date for the composition of this text, as the city was abandoned in the 8th century following the Arab conquest. Nonetheless, the name used for the city is Al-Mada'in which transliterated here.

FRAGMENT II

These are the canons of the churches which the holy fathers (papas), having-assembled [...] in Nicaea, discussed [...], wrote, and established by authority, being eighty[9] [..].

Beloved: when a certain man hath spoken a vow [...], [namely] this Holy Feast[10] which remains on the table. It is simply [...] bread and simply [...] wine [...] and comes out from [...] the church [...] by [...] the Father and the Son and the Holy Ghost in the time of presentation [...] and the arrival of the moment [...].

Verily when a man dedicates an oblation in the church, whether it be wine or whether it be wheat, and the priest does not give one in return, and he says in his heart 'I have not eaten with the priest, I have not drunk with the priest, he hath not reward [...] from heaven in Jerusalem. And God, the possessor [...] of life, withdraweth [...] his light, because he hath desired that which is from earth and refused that which is from heaven, namely the mercies [...] which thy [...] God in his fullness [...] hath granted [...].

Verily a donor [...] having pronounced a vow, namely oblations dedicated in the church, the children of the church shall eat them [...], the Father, the Son and the Holy Ghost come out from [...] the church.

Verily a man having repented [...] in his heart and dedicated an oblation in the church, whether it be wine or wheat or durra-seed[11] down to green vegetables

---

[9] Assumably this is the number of bishops in attendance, which was by tradition 318. This is perhaps an error. Conversely, this number might also refer to the number of canons, which historically were twenty in total. Sometime later, some spurious canons were composed as the so-called Arabic Pseudo-Nicene Canons, which were 80 in total according to Francesco Torres, and 84 according to the Maronite scholar Echellensis Abraham.

[10] The Christian sacrament of the eucharist

[11] That is to say, Sorghum.

[...]; then he, the Lord, will rejoice [...] in his heart and receive [it] through his holy angel.

Have ye not heard that which is written, [...] gift [...] God, him that giveth cheerfully[12] [...] God loveth [...]? All men who work for the name of God' benefit themselves [...], they shall not find benefit [...] through God.

And now therefore. [...] man that which ye do for the name of God, do ye cheerfully. And one was written "men about to [...] become in that [...] shall become covetous, shall become without [...], shall become [...], shall become man-hating, shall become [...], shall become covetous of the priesthood[13]." And all this . . . beloved, enquire ye unwillingly. Let us have friendship, let us seek peace, and when ye sit enquire ye with desire (?), because coveting ye are fearful of death. Without ceasing, let us pray to God that he may give us remission of our sins.

Behold, hear ye a witness- Verily a layman (ⲗⲁⲓⲕⲟⲥ)[14] having [...] and eaten the food of the church, he shall [...] the priest [...] and shall [...] And now therefore [...] enquire ye in [...] requital [...] in desire enquire ye.

And when thou hast sat down remain far from the feast. And when thou hast received the feast, purify thy heart and voice and come and receive the feast. And verily if not, it is destruction.

Verily, if thou comest not at peace with a teaching man thou art a feast-taker.

Verily, when thou desirest to receive the feast, come out first and come in good will. Verily, if thou art not in good, [you] will remain outside the church: wilt

---

[12] This appears to be a mangled quote from 2 Cor. 9:7-8
[13] Likewise, this appears to be 2 Tim. 3:2
[14] Presumably this refers to the laity refusing communion from the priest, which was a more common ecclesiastical habit in the first millenia.

thou [...] through God be friendly[15]? And if not, thus wilt thou [...] and [...] the laws of God?

And when thou hast received the feast, remain in the church till the dismissal. Remember what was done to Judas the betrayer: having taken the feast he went out of the church not having been dismissed, and Satan entered into his heart and persuaded him to betray[16].

In truth, thou also, when the church has not been dismissed, art [...]. It is that which God shall take as cause and requite upon thee. Be not condemned for eternity with Judas on account of the short moment after this.

I have seen many when they have received the sacrament eat when the church is not open: woe to their hearts! Shall they receive in exchange [for] remission of sin, because they were able to [...]?

Verily, a donor who has eaten when the church was not open, he hath cause in a great [...]

Verily, a donor who has eaten and received the sacrament, loveth light with the eater of the dead[17].

A donor who not hearing the epistle and gospel hath, received the sacrament, hath not received.

A donor who hath not sung alleluia with the singers[18] insidteth God his Maker, for 'Alleluia' is 'Thelkath Marimath'[19]. And the saying, being interpreted is "Let us glorify God who founded all (things) and let us love and worship him."

---

[15] Griffith suggests as an alternative "art thou greater than God?"
[16] This passage has a parallel in a homily of Eusebius of Alexandria (XVI.2, On the day of the Lord)
[17] Griffith suggests as an alternative "the dead body produces light to the eater".
[18] That is, with the Psalmist

Woe be to the man who speaketh in the church at the time of the sacrament![20] For he that speaketh in the church at the time of the sacrament is negligent more than all the negligent ones. For the man that speaketh in the church is the enemy of God. For these are like the Jews who hung the Saviour on the cross, [and] mocked him — they who speak when this sacrament is upon the table. He, the Lord it is who hath said "and the Jews alone openly rejected me."[21] And you who speak in the church at all times, behold, hearken ye to the warning.[22]

Verily, one [who is] dedicating [their] oblation in the church, by means of the act of service of life, he shall write his name in Jerusalem. And his reward with the priest here is one loaf (ⲁⲡⲧⲟⲩ), and one finger[23] of wine. For this is what was taken by God.

Woe be to the priest who sitteth on the Lord's Day (ⲕⲩⲣⲓⲁⲕⲏ) amongst [...]one by [...] departing and eating will requite that one sin upon the scalp of the dead of the priest in the fullness of the ages. And all persons, either having become a woman [or] being 12 years old shall give or having become a man being 13 years old shall give. And [...] and verily he who hath [...] one of these, is good both in the [...] of the flesh and the [...] of the [...] and God will try [taxing] his soul in hell.

---

[19] A phrase of unknown origin that appears elsewhere. This appears in the Apocalypse of St. Bartholomew along with only unknown, vaguely Aramiac statements which are intended to relate directly to Christ's divinity. It has been suggested that this is intended to mean something akin to 'Let us glorify God'. Similar phraseologies are also found in the Apocalypse of Paul, which is more pronounced in the Latin versions of the same text.

[20] The act of consecration, which then as now, was intended to be a numinous event.

[21] This does not appear in the Christian scriptures, but it might relate to Luke 9:22

[22] Griffith suggests from this section that this is not a copy of the Arabic Pseudo-Nicene canons, but a sermon sourced from them about the proper behavior in church.

[23] The Old Nubian word that is used here appears (ϯⲁⲣⲡⲏ) to be a loan or a transliteration of the Arabic.

Therefore, praise God. Praise be Thine! In the hand of the living God 1 will overcome and expel!

And the priest each Lord's Day shall cause them to hear this: for it hath been done, that we may attain resurrection and grace with our Lord Jesus Christ, to whom belongs the glory and the power unto ages of ages! Amen.

The Scriptorium Project is the work of a small group of lay people of various apostolic churches who are interested in the preservation, transmission, and translation of the works of the early and medieval church. Our efforts are to make the works of the church fathers accessible to anyone who might have an interest in Christian antiquities and the theological, philosophical, and moral writings that have become the bedrock of Western Civilization.

To-date, our releases have pulled from the Greek, Syriac, Georgian, Latin, Celtic, Ethiopian, and Coptic traditions of Christianity, and have been pulled from sundry local traditions and languages.

Other Titles and Translations by D.P. Curtin:

Lebor Gabala Erenn by Nennius the Monk (2017)
The Eight Vices by Eutropis of Valencia (2017)
Three Letters from the Companion of the Bulgars by St. Rupert of Juvavum (2017)
Privileges of the Abbot of Canterbury by St. Augustine of Canterbury (2017)
Nicene Canons in the Old Nubian Language (2018)
Apology to Gunthamund, King of Vandals by Aemeilius Dracontius (2018)
First Book of Ethiopian Maccabees (2018)
Chronicon: a short chronicle of Visigothic Spain by Eutrandus of Ticino (2019)
Decrees of Aethelbert by St. Aethelbert, King of Kent (2019)
The Measure to be taxed for Penance by St. Columba of Iona (2019)
Protoevangelium of James: Greek and English Texts (2019)
Edicts of the Synod of Paris by Chlothar II, King of Franks (2019)
The Life of St. Desiderius by Sisebut, King of Visigoths (2019)
The Synod of Rome by St. Boniface IV of Rome (2019)
Letter to Pope Theodore by Victor of Carthage (2020)
The Decree of 610 by Gundemar, King of Visigoths (2020)
Laws of the Church by Chlothar III, King of Franks (2020)
Donations by St. Aethelbert, King of Kent (2020)
The Mystical Interpretation by St. Aileran the Wise (2020)
Laws of the Church by St. Dagobert II, King of Franks (2020)
The Old Nubian Miracle of St. Mena (2021)
About Fifteen Problems by St. Albertus Magnus (2022)
Testament of Some Former Things by John Scotus Eriugena (2022)
The Georgian Synaxarium (2022)
Instructions: Counsel for Novices by St. Ammonas the Hermit (2022)
The Syriac Menologium and Martyrology (2022)
Book on Religious Exercise and Quiet by St. Isaiah the Solitary (2022)
Vision of Theophilus by St. Cyril of Alexandria (2022)
On Fate (De Fato) by St. Albertus Magnus (2023)
Fragments of 'Chronicle' by Hippolytus of Thebes (2023)
Life of the Blessed Theotokos by Epiphanius Monachus (2023)
Syriac Life of John the Baptist by Serapion the Presbyter (2023)
Second Book of Ethiopian Maccabees (2023)